1·2·3
I Can Draw!

Irene Luxbacher

KIDS CAN PRESS

A drawing is a **PICTURE** you make with pencils, colored pencils, crayons, markers or chalk. It can look like something real or something you imagine. Let's draw people …

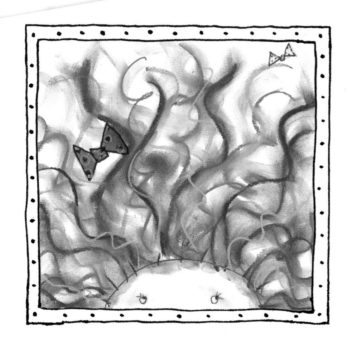

The things you use to make a drawing are called
MATERIALS.

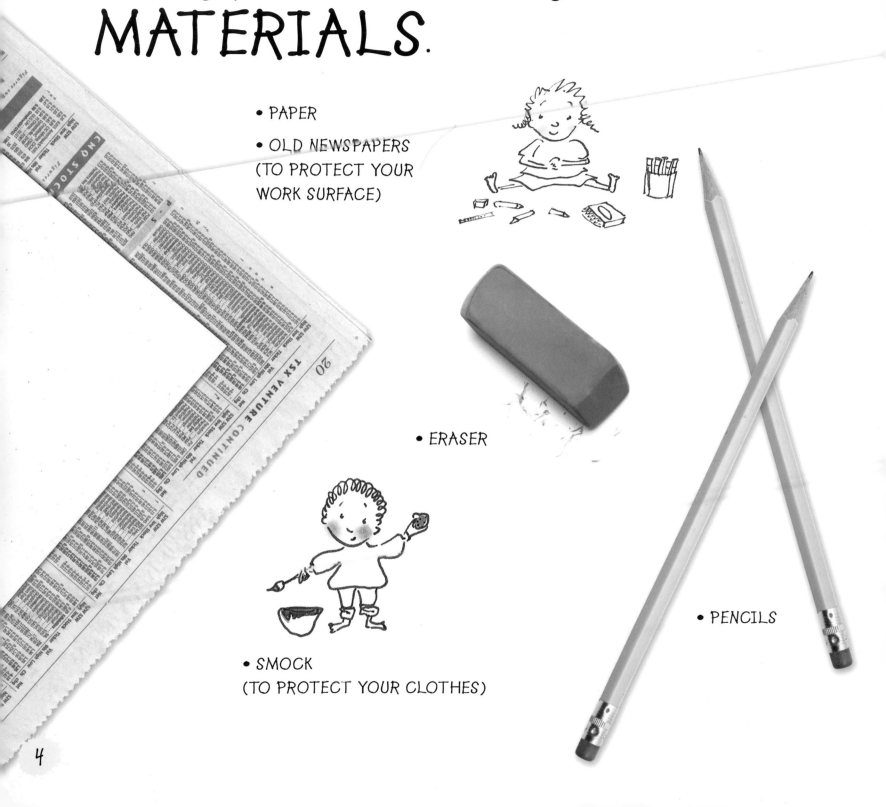

- PAPER

- OLD NEWSPAPERS
(TO PROTECT YOUR
WORK SURFACE)

- ERASER

- SMOCK
(TO PROTECT YOUR CLOTHES)

- PENCILS

• COLORED PENCILS

• WASHABLE MARKERS

• COLORED CHALK

• CRAYONS

ARTIST SECRET:

If you want to make dark or thick marks on your paper, use a drawing tool that has a big or soft tip.

If you want to make light or thin marks on your paper, use a drawing tool that has a sharp or hard tip.

5

LINE Up

Draw a picture of a wild head of hair that you make with LOTS and LOTS of different LINES!

1. Use a pencil or piece of colored chalk to draw a half circle at the bottom of your page. This will be the top of your drawing's face.

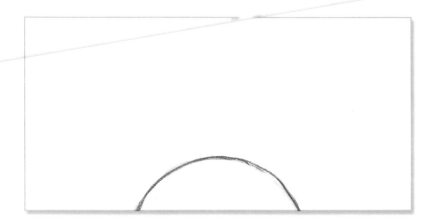

2. Fill your page with lots of colorful chalk lines growing from the head. Your lines can be straight, curly, wavy … whatever you think looks like a wild head of hair.

3. Rub or smudge some of your chalk lines with your finger or a piece of tissue. This will make the lines look fuzzy.

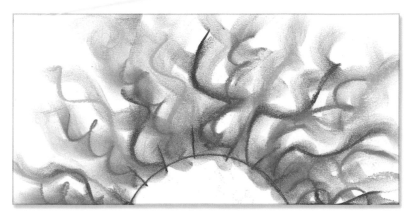

YIKES!
A Hairy Business!

Use a pencil to draw two eyes. Add colorful ribbons, clips or a hat to your amazing hairdo using colored pencils or markers. Or turn your page upside down and draw a smile below the eyes so your hairy picture becomes a long and woolly beard.

A drawing can be made with lots of different kinds of lines. LINES are LONG MARKS you make on a page. They can be

THICK

THIN

STRAIGHT

WAVY

ZIGZAG

CURLY

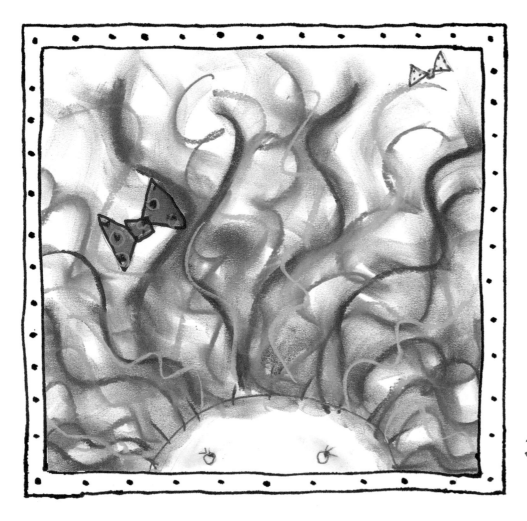

Getting into SHAPES

CIRCLES, SQUARES, OVALS, TRIANGLES, RECTANGLES … By putting together a few different shapes, you can draw a whole gallery of royal pictures!

1. Use a pencil to draw a rectangle. Draw a small square on top of the rectangle. Draw an oval on top of the square. These are the shoulders, neck and head of your drawing of a king or queen.

2. Draw a face by adding small ovals for eyes and ears, a small triangle for a nose and small rectangles for eyebrows and a mouth. You can also draw straight, curly or wavy lines to add some royal hair.

3. Add a crown and necklace by drawing a row of small triangles across the head and neck. Decorate the crown and necklace with jewels made of very small squares and circles.

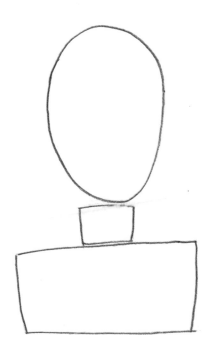

HEAR YE, HEAR YE!
Presenting a Royal Court!

Try making a few more drawings by using different shapes and shape sizes. Use markers to draw fancy frames around each of your drawings to make a gallery of queens, kings, princes and princesses.

One way to start a drawing is to use simple SHAPES:

CIRCLES

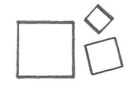

SQUARES

OVALS

TRIANGLES

RECTANGLES

9

EXPRESS Yourself

You can tell a lot about how people are FEELING by looking at their mouths and eyebrows. Draw some underwater adventurers and discover how to make FACES that are happy, sad, angry and surprised.

1. Use a pencil to draw four large circles in a row, leaving some space in between. In each circle, draw two dots for eyes and a small half circle for a nose.

2. Add a different mouth for each face. Draw a line that curves up on the first face, a line that curves down on the second face, a wavy line on the third face and a small circle on the fourth face.

3. Add different eyebrows for each face. Draw two lines that curve down on the first face, two straight lines that point down on the second face, two lines that curve up on the third face and two lines that curve down high above the eyes on the last face.

BLUB, BLUB!
What a Ride!

First, draw circles around each face for windows. Next draw one large, long oval around all of the windows to make a submarine. Then add two or three small ovals at one end of your submarine for a propeller. Use colorful markers or chalk to draw sea creatures and color in the deep blue sea.

The **EXPRESSION** on someone's face shows you how he or she is feeling. Look at yourself in the mirror — how many expressions can you make?

11

BODY Basics

When you draw a person's body, how do all the **PARTS** of their **BODY** fit together? Count down the different parts while you draw an **ASTRONAUT** who is ready to blast off into outer space!

1. Use a pencil to draw three circles: one for your astronaut's waist, a larger one for the chest and a smaller one for the head.

2. Draw six ovals for your astronaut's legs: two large ovals under the waist for thighs, one smaller oval under each thigh for shins and one small oval at the bottom of each shin for feet.

3. Draw six more ovals for arms: two ovals on either side of the chest for upper arms, one smaller oval at the end of each upper arm for lower arms and one small oval at the bottom of each lower arm for hands.

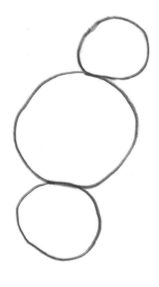

ZOOM!
An Out-of-This-World Astronaut!

When you draw a picture of a whole body, it is called a FIGURE DRAWING.

Draw a square inside your astronaut's head to finish the helmet. Add five small ovals to the end of each hand to look like the fingers of gloves. Use markers to draw yellow stars and color a purple or black sky. Now your astronaut is floating in outer space!

Get MOVING

Have you ever noticed that you bend your knees when you jump? What else does your body do when it moves? Try drawing **AMAZING ACROBATS** that flip and fly through the air!

1. Use a pencil to draw a standing stick figure. Draw dots at the figure's knees and elbows. Draw another dot where the legs of your stick figure meet the body for the figure's waist.

2. Draw another stick figure like the one in step 1, this one bending at its knees, elbows and waist.

3. Turn your page upside down, and draw another stick figure that bends at the knees, elbows and waist.

WOW!
A Circus of Acrobats!

Draw over your amazing acrobats' bodies with crayons, colored pencils or chalk to give them colorful costumes. Use a marker or pencil to draw in their hair and faces. How about drawing a trapeze or trampoline for your acrobats to swing or bounce on? Whee!

By changing the POSITIONS of its arms and legs, you can make a figure drawing that looks like it's moving.

Trying on TEXTURES

Here's a drawing project that looks like it would feel! First collect a few flat things from around the house that you like the feel of, such as BUMPY fabric, ROUGH sandpaper or a WRINKLED paper bag.

1. Use a pencil to draw a stick figure.

2. Use a dark crayon to draw some warm, wintry clothes around the figure. How about a woolly hat and mitts, a fuzzy winter coat and warm corduroy pants?

3. To give the clothes some TEXTURE, put your drawing over one of the pieces you collected. Rub the paper with the side of a piece of colored chalk or a crayon until you see the texture come through. Try this with the other things you've collected using different colored chalk or crayons until all the clothes have texture and color.

MMM... Toasty Warm!

Use a marker or pencil to draw a face and add some hair. What else does your well-dressed friend need? Use colored pencils or markers to add details like pink cheeks, big boots and anything else you think a person would wear on a winter day.

The way something feels when you touch it is called TEXTURE. A drawing can look like it has texture.

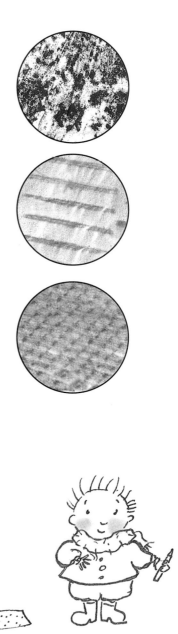

Hey, WHO'S THAT?

Imagine what you would look like if you could be **ANYTHING** you wanted to be. Would you be a pirate? A ballerina? A musician? A superhero? Now use your **DRAWING** know-how to make a **SELF-PORTRAIT**. Start by taking a good long look at yourself in the mirror.

POSITION

Think about what position your body will be in. Will you be sitting? Standing? Running? Jumping? Use a pencil to draw a simple stick figure in that position.

FIGURE

Draw circles and ovals over your stick figure to fill out your body parts: a chest, a waist, upper and lower arms, upper and lower legs, then hands and feet.

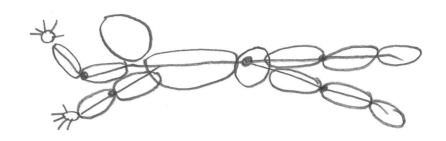

GETTING DRESSED

Draw the clothes or costume you will wear. Add some texture by placing your drawing over a flat object, like corduroy fabric, a woolly sweater or a shaggy carpet. Rub the side of a piece of colored chalk or a crayon over your drawing until the texture comes through.

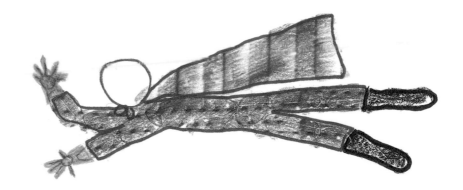

FACE

Start with some simple shapes to draw your face. Are your eyes more like ovals or circles? Is your nose like a long triangle or a short one? Draw ovals for your ears and two circles beside your triangle nose for nostrils.

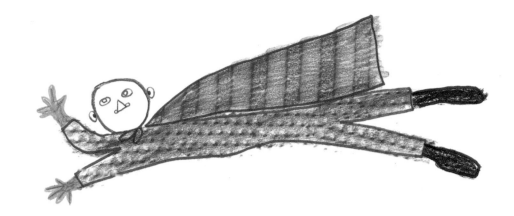

EXPRESSION

Do you want your self-portrait to look happy, sad or maybe surprised? Eyebrows that curve down and a mouth that's smiling make your face look happy. Eyebrows that are straight and a mouth that's frowning make your face look sad. Eyebrows that curve up and a mouth that looks like a circle will look surprised.

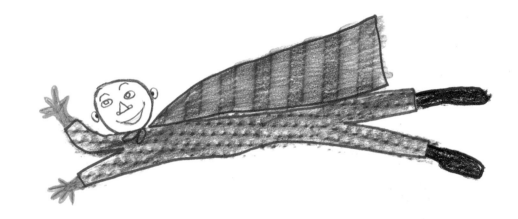

HAIR

Do you have curly hair or straight hair? Is it long or short? Draw lots of lines growing from the top of your head using a thick pencil or piece of chalk. Use your finger or a tissue to smudge some of your lines together.

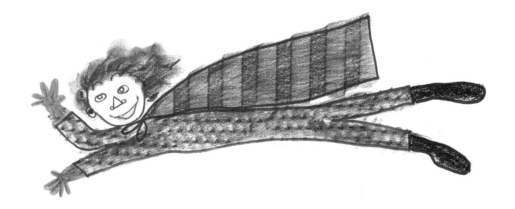

TA-DA!
A Masterpiece That Is ME!

Use crayons and markers to finish your drawing by adding more color to your clothes or costume. Draw in your favorite jewelry, your glasses, your lucky shoes or anything else you wear that makes you really you.

A **PORTRAIT** is a picture of a real person. A picture you make of yourself is called a **SELF-PORTRAIT**.

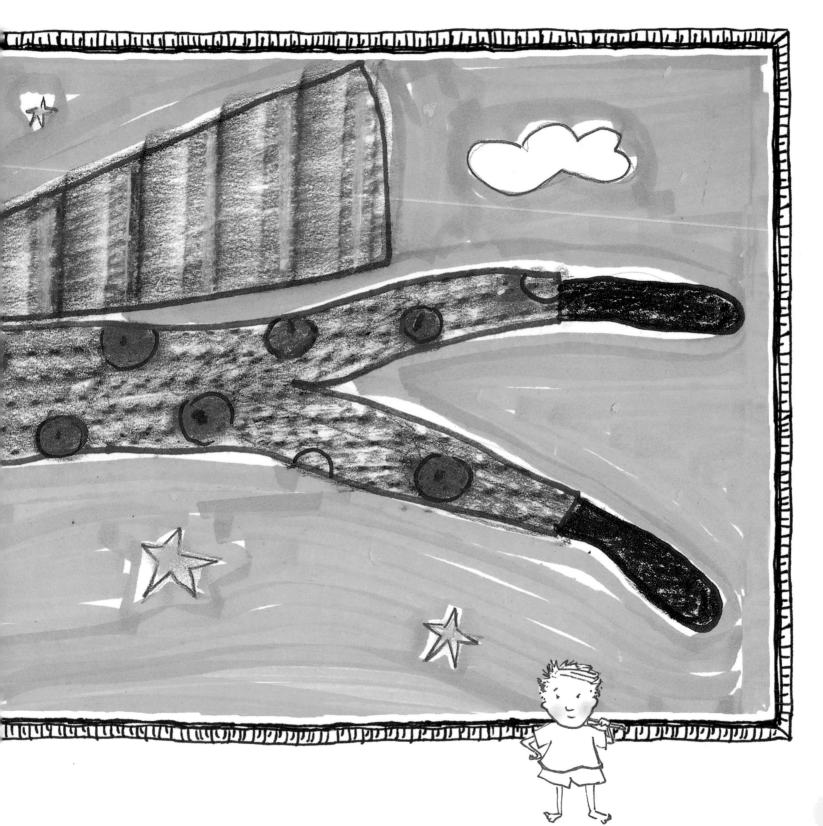

21

Note to PARENTS and TEACHERS

We chose to use people as a fun theme for exploring some basic drawing techniques, but there are lots of other themes you can use as inspiration for your young artist. Here are some ideas to get you started.

- Fill a page with a sketch of a snake. Start with a squiggly line drawn with a colored pencil or marker for the twisting, turning snake's body (see Line Up, page 6). Add the head, eyes, nostrils and tongue using some basic shapes (see Getting into Shapes, page 8). Give the snake an expression by drawing in eyebrows and a mouth (see Express Yourself, page 10). Rub some textured scales on to the snake's body using colorful chalk (see Trying on Textures, page 16).

- Or be blown away by drawing some wild weather. Use thick pencils or markers to draw the spiraling, scribbled lines of a tornado and the bold zigzags of lightning bolts (see Line Up, page 6). Put together simple shapes to make a scene with a house, trees and cars (see Getting into Shapes, page 8). Add stick figures bent over in different positions walking into the blowing winds (see Get Moving, page 14).

Tips to ensure a GOOD DRAWING EXPERIENCE every time:

1. Use inexpensive materials and make sure your young artist's clothes and the work surface are protected from marks and scribbles. This way it's all about the fun, not about the waste and the mess.

2. Focus on the process, rather than the product. Make sure your young artist is relaxed and having fun with the information, instead of expecting perfection every time. The truth is, learning to draw comes with time and practice.

3. Remind your young artist that mistakes are an artist's best friend. The most interesting drawing ideas or techniques are often discovered by mistake.

DRAWING Words

EXPRESSION
page 11

LINE
page 7

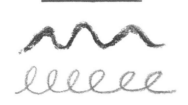

POSITIONS
page 15

FIGURE DRAWING
page 13

MATERIALS
page 4

PORTRAIT
page 20

SELF-PORTRAIT
page 20

SHAPES
page 9

TEXTURE
page 17

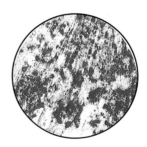

23

FOR ELIJAH AND NOAH

Special thanks to Stacey Roderick and Karen Powers. This book would not have been possible without their amazing talents and insights.

Text and illustrations © 2008 Irene Luxbacher

Edited by Stacey Roderick
Designed by Karen Powers

Photos on pages 4–5: pencils © iStockphoto.com, pie plate © iStockphoto.com/Jose Gil, sponges © iStockphoto.com/Bill Noll, eraser © iStockphoto.com/Christine Balderas
Printed and bound in Singapore

The hardcover edition of this book is smyth sewn casebound. The paperback edition of this book is limp sewn with a drawn-on cover.

CM 08   0 9 8 7 6 5 4 3 2 1
CM PA 08   0 9 8 7 6 5 4 3 2 1

Kids Can Press acknowledges the financial support of the Government of Ontario, through the Ontario Media Development Corporation's Ontario Book Initiative, and the Government of Canada, through the BPIDP, for our publishing activity.

Published in Canada by
Kids Can Press Ltd.
29 Birch Avenue
Toronto, ON M4V 1E2

Published in the U.S. by
Kids Can Press Ltd.
2250 Military Road
Tonawanda, NY 14150

www.kidscanpress.com

Kids Can Press is a **corus**™ Entertainment company

Library and Archives Canada Cataloguing in Publication

Luxbacher, Irene, 1970–
    123 I can draw! / Irene Luxbacher.

(Starting art)
ISBN 978-1-55453-039-7 (bound)
ISBN 978-1-55453-152-3 (pbk.)

1. Drawing—Technique—Juvenile literature. I. Title.
II. Title: One, two, three I can draw! III. Series: Luxbacher,
Irene, 1970– Starting art.

NC655.L89 2008   j741.2   C2007-902727-X